Listen · Read · Think
SCIENCE

How Does it Grow?
From Seed to Sunflower

Ian Smith

Teacher Created Resources

Published in the United States by
QEB Publishing, Inc.
23062 La Cadena Drive
Laguna Hills, CA 92653

This edition published by
Teacher Created Resources, Inc.
6421 Industry Way
Westminster, CA 92683

www.teachercreated.com

Library of Congress Control Number 2004102033

ISBN 978-1-4206-8120-8

Written by Ian Smith
Designed by Zeta Davies
Editor Hannah Ray
Picture Researcher Joanne Beardwell
Illustrated by Chris Davidson

Series Consultant Anne Faundez
Creative Director Louise Morley
Editorial Manager Jean Coppendale

Printed and bound in China

Picture credits
Key: t = top, b = bottom, c = center, l = left, r = right
Corbis Dennis Blachut 12/ Becky Lulgart–Stayner 16/ Owaki–Kulla 9/ Tom Stewart 8/ Jim Sugar 14/ Ron Watts 11; **Ecoscene** Papilio Robert Picket 6t, 6c, 6b, 7, 13; **Gettyimages** Davies & Star 4c, 22t/ John Lawrence 10/ Rita Maas 4t/ Steve Satushek 5/ Paul Vlant 17.

Contents

How does it grow?

The sunflower grows from a seed. Inside this seed is a tiny plant. The seed also contains the food that the tiny plant needs to help it grow.

The sunflower seed starts to grow, or **germinate**, in the spring when the weather is warm and the soil is damp. After a few days, a root pushes its way out of the seed.

The root grows down into the ground and holds the new plant in the soil.

The root takes water and **minerals** from the soil.

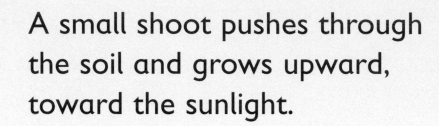

A small shoot pushes through
the soil and grows upward,
toward the sunlight.

The little plant is now
called a seedling.

Then, the stem
starts to grow.

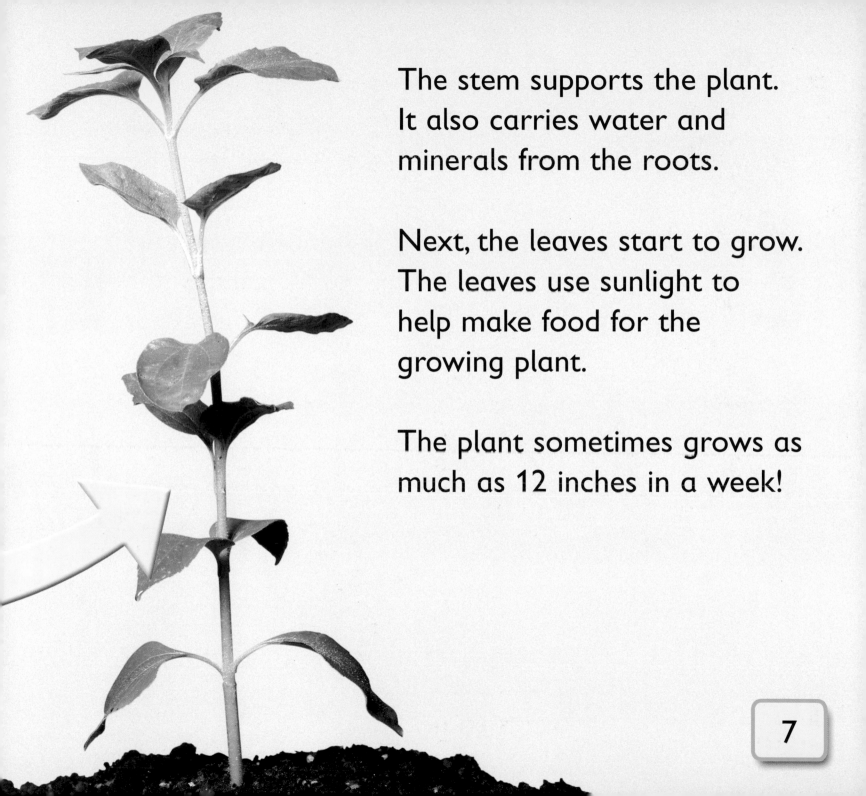

The stem supports the plant. It also carries water and minerals from the roots.

Next, the leaves start to grow. The leaves use sunlight to help make food for the growing plant.

The plant sometimes grows as much as 12 inches in a week!

Sunflower sizes

To grow big and strong, the sunflower needs air, water, and lots of sunshine.

Sunflowers can grow up to ten feet tall. This is one and a half times as tall as a very tall person!

Sunflower plants are fully grown
after about three months.

Flowers in bloom

The sunflower plant makes flowers. What looks like a large flower is really many small flowers.

The flowers in the middle are like short tubes.

The tube-like flowers at the edge each have a yellow **petal**.

The sunflower needs
a lot of sunshine.

The head of the
sunflower turns
to face the sun all
through the day.

11

Sunflower seeds

Sunflower seeds come from the flowers.

As the flowers die, the petals fall off. But a seed begins to grow inside each flower.

You can see the new seeds when the flower turns brown, after the petals have fallen off.

The seeds fall to the ground.

They lie on the ground until the following spring.

Then, when the soil is warm and **moist**, the seeds germinate and start to grow again.

Good to eat

Sunflower seeds are used for food.

They are very good for you. They help you to grow strong and healthy.

Roasted seeds make a delicious snack!

Sunflower oil is made from sunflower seeds. It is used in cooking and in salads.

How to grow a sunflower

What you need:
- Sunflower seeds
- Compost
- 4-inch pots

What to do:
Fill the pots with moist compost.

Make two holes in the compost, 1 inch deep.

Drop a seed into each hole and cover it over with moist compost.

Place the pots in a warm room and keep the compost moist, but not wet.

After a few days, the seedlings will start to grow!

Planting the seedlings

Make holes, about 12 inches apart, in the soil.

Turn the pots upside down and gently tip out the seedlings.

Drop the seedlings into the holes.

Make sure that you press the soil down firmly around the roots.

Water the seedlings at least once a week if the weather is dry.

Watch your sunflower plants grow!

Glossary

Germinate—when a seed starts to grow and develop.

Minerals—substances that plants take up from the soil with their roots and use to help them grow.

Moist—slightly damp.

Petal—the parts of a flower that are often brightly colored.

Index

Parents' and teachers' notes

- Explain that this book is nonfiction and that it has a contents page, a glossary, and an index.
- Explain the purpose of the index (to locate information) and the glossary (to explain difficult or technical words in the text).
- Talk about the name of the flower and its link with the sun.
- Explain that the first part of the book is all about how a sunflower grows, and that the second part gives simple instructions for growing your own sunflower.
- Explain the word "seed" as the very beginning of a flower's life. Emphasize that air, water, and warmth are essential to make the tiny plant grow.
- Draw a picture of a sunflower and label its parts—root, stem, leaves, flower, and petals.
- Explain that all living things grow and that the plant grows just as children grow—but a lot faster!
- After reading through pages 6–7 together, find out what 12 inches looks like, using a ruler.

- Look at the photograph of the sunflower on page 10. How many petals can your child count? What color are the petals?
- Show the inside of an apple to your child, and point out the seeds. Warn your child that not all seeds are good to eat like those of the sunflower.
- Look at the word "sunflower." Count the number of times the word "sunflower" appears throughout the book.
- Together, follow the step-by-step instructions for growing a sunflower.
- Hold a competition for your child and his/her friends to see whose sunflower grows the tallest.
- Grow another fast-growing plant from seed, e.g. a green bean. Together, note down each stage of the plant's development under the heading, "How does it grow?"
- Help your child to write a set of instructions explaining how to grow the new plant.